UNITED STATES
the people

Martha Morss

A Bobbie Kalman Book

The Lands, Peoples, and Cultures Series

 Crabtree Publishing Company

www.crabtreebooks.com

The Lands, Peoples, and Cultures Series
Created by Bobbie Kalman

Author: Martha Morss

Editor: Lynn Peppas

Proofreader: Rachel Eagen

Photo research: Crystal Sikkens, Planman Technologies

Editorial director: Kathy Middleton

Design: Planman Technologies

Production coordinator: Margaret Amy Salter

Prepress technician: Margaret Amy Salter

Print coordinator: Katherine Berti

Written, developed, and produced by Planman Technologies

Cover: Students face the American flag and recite The Pledge of Allegiance in their school library.

Title page: Large Crowd of People Holding Stars and Stripes Flags

Back cover: Bald Eagle

Icon: Statue of Liberty

Illustrations:
Bonna Rouse: back cover

Photographs:
Corbis: © Richard A. Cooke: p. 6; © Marilyn Angel Wynn/ Nativestock Pictures: p. 8 (bl); © BLUE LANTERN STUDIO / LAUGHING E/Blue Lantern Studio: 10 (b); © David Butow: 18 (b); © Holly Kuper/AgStock Images: 20 (b)
istockphoto: front cover, p. 22 (l), 24 (b)
Library of Congress: p. 11 (tl), 12, 13, 14 (b), 15 (l), 16 (l)
Shutterstock: p. 7 (t), 9 (tr), 10 (t), 17 (t), 18 (t), 19 (t), 20 (t), 24 (t), 30, 31; Christopher Halloran: p. 5 (t); Jose Gil: p. 7 (b); Kathy Burns-Millyard: p. 21 (b); carroteater: p. 25 (t); Domenic Gareri: p. 25 (b); Alexey Stiop: p. 26 (tl); Jeff Schultes: p. 26 (br)
Thinkstock: title page, p. 3, 4, 5 (b), 9 (b), 16 (r), 19 (b), 22 (r), 23, 27, 28, 29
Wikimedia Commons: p. 9 (tl); Library of Congress: p. 8 (br), 14 (t); The Bancroft Library: p. 11 (tr); Bedford: p. 11 (b); U.S. National Archives and Records Administration: 15 (r); Carl: p. 17 (b); soldiersmediacenter: p. 21 (t)

Every effort has been made to obtain the appropriate credit and full copyright clearance for all images in this book. Any oversights, despite Crabtree's greatest precautions, will be corrected in future editions.

Library and Archives Canada Cataloguing in Publication

Morss, Martha
    United States : the people / Martha Morss.

(The lands, peoples, and cultures series)
Includes index.
Issued also in electronic formats.
ISBN 978-0-7787-9836-1 (bound).--ISBN 978-0-7787-9839-2 (pbk.)

    1. United States--Social conditions--Juvenile literature.
2. Immigrants--United States--Juvenile literature. I. Title.
II. Series: Lands, peoples, and cultures series

HN57.M67 2012   j973   C2012-902713-8

Library of Congress Cataloging-in-Publication Data

Morss, Martha.
    United States the people / Martha Morss.
        p. cm. -- (The lands, peoples, and cultures series)
    Includes index.
    ISBN 978-0-7787-9836-1 (reinforced library binding : alk. paper) -- ISBN 978-0-7787-9839-2 (pbk. : alk. paper) -- ISBN 978-1-4271-7895-4 (electronic pdf : alk. paper) -- ISBN 978-1-4271-8010-0 (electronic html : alk. paper)
    1. Immigrants--United States--Juvenile literature. 2. United States--Social life and customs--Juvenile literature. I. Title.

    JV6465.M67 2012
    973--dc23
                                        2012016095

Crabtree Publishing Company

Printed in Canada/102012/MA20120817

www.crabtreebooks.com   1-800-387-7650

Published in Canada
Crabtree Publishing
616 Welland Ave.
St. Catharines, Ontario
L2M 5V6

Published in the United States
Crabtree Publishing
PMB 59051
350 Fifth Avenue, 59th Floor
New York, New York 10118

Published in the United Kingdom
Crabtree Publishing
Maritime House
Basin Road North, Hove
BN41 1WR

Published in Australia
Crabtree Publishing
3 Charles Street
Coburg North
VIC, 3058

Contents

 # Land of liberty

If there are just two words that sum up the United States today, those words are probably liberty and diversity. That's because ever since the nation's birth, in 1776, Americans have valued freedom and they have welcomed people from other countries all over the world.

Today, one way that Americans exercise their freedom is by voting. They elect a president for the whole nation and a governor for their state. They also elect national, state, and local lawmakers. In these ways, as Civil War president Abraham Lincoln said, the United States has a government "of the people, by the people, for the people."

A diverse people

The United States has been a magnet for people from every part of the world because it stands for freedom. In addition to being very diverse, the United States is very large. It reaches from the Atlantic Ocean to the Pacific Ocean, from Mexico to Canada. Its 50 states include one

northwest of Canada (Alaska) and one far out in the Pacific Ocean (Hawaii). The United States also has a great many people. It ranks third in population in the world.

Birth of a nation

Before the United States existed, the land was home to scattered groups of native peoples. Gradually, between about 1500 and 1700, European explorers arrived. In 1492 Christopher Columbus sailed from Spain and met natives living on small islands southwest of Florida. Later explorers met Native Americans in the East, the Southwest, and the Mississippi Valley.

People from Great Britain became the most numerous settlers in the new land. By 1733, there were 13 English **colonies** along the eastern seaboard. Eventually, the colonies found British rule too limiting. They broke away to form a new country, the United States, and fought a war with Britain, called the American Revolution, to defend their independence.

(top) The Statue of Liberty was a gift to the United States from the people of France in 1886, on the 100th anniversary of the American Revolution.

Born in Hawaii, Barack Obama served as both an Illinois state senator and a United States senator. In 2008 he was elected President of the United States. His ancestors came from England, Ireland, and Kenya.

(below) Today, the American population is diverse and vibrant.

The Constitution

After winning freedom from Great Britain, American leaders debated what kind of government they should have. They created something new, a strong central government with three branches: a president; the Congress, made up of two groups of lawmakers; and a judiciary, or system of judges. The structure and powers of the national government are spelled out in the U.S. Constitution. This document also states important rights guaranteed to all Americans.

Americans at a glance

Number of states: 50
Population in 2010: 308,745,538
—**People under age 18:** 24 percent
Most widely spoken language: English
—**People who speak a different language at home:** 19 percent
Ethnic/racial background (percent):
—White (not Hispanic), 64
—Hispanic (of any race), 16
—Black, 12
—Asian, 4
—Persons reporting two or more races, 3
—American Indian, 1
—Pacific Islander, less than 1

The first Americans

Some 20,000 years ago, during the Ice Age, North America was joined to Asia in the far north by a strip of land. Early hunters from Asia crossed this land bridge into what is now Alaska and Canada. Very slowly, they migrated south. By the time the ice sheets melted, about 11,000 years ago, groups of Native Americans were living throughout the area now called the United States.

The mound builders

The ancient mound builders lived mainly in wooded river valleys east of the Mississippi River. At their settlements they built large **earthworks**. These vary in size, shape, and arrangement. Some look like simple cones or flat-topped hills. Others are more complex. For example, at Poverty Point, in Louisiana, the mounds form six ridges arranged in a semicircle about three-fourths of a mile (1.2 kilometers) long. Originally about five feet (1.5 meters) high, the mounds were built by carrying loads of dirt in woven baskets.

The mounds had different purposes. Some were used for burying the dead and their belongings. Others were platforms for temples or houses. Mound-building peoples existed at different times roughly between 1000 BCE and 1600 CE.

The Anasazi

Today's Pueblo of the western United States trace their origin to the Anasazi. Their culture developed around 1200 bce in the region where the corners of Colorado, Utah, New Mexico, and Arizona meet. At first the Anasazi lived in shallow pit houses underground. Later, they built above-ground houses with stone walls. These houses evolved into apartment-like dwellings made of stone and dried mud. The Anasazi were farmers and traders, and they had contacts with groups of Native Americans in Mexico and what is now California.

(below) Serpent Mound, in southern Ohio, was probably built by people of the Adena culture and may have been used for special ceremonies. Today, it is a National Historic Landmark.

(above) These tourists are exploring Cliff Palace at Mesa Verde National Park in New Mexico. More than 100 ancestral Puebloans lived in the 150 rooms of the palace.

Encounters with Europeans

The Pueblo were one of the first Native American groups to meet European explorers, when Spanish conquistadors, or conquerors, came to the region. Eastern **tribes** such as the Pequot, Iroquois, and Cherokee encountered English colonists. The Europeans were interested in land and resources from the land, such as furs. At first Europeans befriended and traded with the Native Americans, but conflicts soon developed. Many Native Americans died in early wars with the settlers. Many more died from diseases, such as smallpox, brought to North America by Europeans.

Way of life

The food, clothing, and shelter of Native American tribes varied, depending on the environment where they lived. For example, tribes of the western Plains were **nomadic**, moving from place to place to hunt. They built tent-like homes of buffalo skins laid over poles. These homes were easy to build and easy to move. In eastern forests, the Iroquois built long rectangular houses from logs. Each tribe had its own kind of government, often led by one or more chiefs. In all parts of the country, Native Americans who lived in settlements hunted wildlife and grew vegetables such as corn and squash.

(right) Pow wows are festive gatherings that celebrate Native American heritage. Young and old gather to dance, sing, and pass traditions from generation to generation.

From the beginning, people of both English and African heritage lived side by side in Great Britain's North American colonies. Most English arrived as free persons. Nearly all Africans, however, came to the New World involuntarily, as slaves. Sadly, this stark inequality between whites and African Americans lasted through 250 years of American history. The number of free African Americans was very small, but it grew somewhat during the colonial period.

Some colonists came to North America as indentured servants. These were poor people who agreed to work for a master for a certain period of time in return for transportation to North America. At the end of that time, often seven years, indentured servants were granted their freedom.

Virginia

The first permanent English settlement in North America was called Jamestown, in the colony of Virginia. About 100 colonists arrived in three ships in 1607, during the reign of Queen Elizabeth I. Their goal was to claim land for Great Britain and search for gold and other valuable resources.

The Virginia colony struggled at first—with disease, lack of food and fresh water, and occasional attacks by Native Americans. More than half of the colonists died. After more settlers came, an all-out war with the native Powhatans ended in a truce. Again the colony struggled.

After 1618, things improved when leaders set up a body of legislators, or lawmakers, like those in England. By this time, the Virginia colonists had begun to grow tobacco for **export** to the Mother Country, England. In 1619, the first Africans arrived on a ship from Angola. They were promptly put to work in the tobacco fields.

The mystery of Roanoke
Jamestown was more successful than an earlier Virginia colony at Roanoke. Begun unsuccessfully in 1585, a new group of about 100 settlers landed in 1587. Within three years the colony mysteriously disappeared. Early records tell us that a baby girl, named Virginia Dare, was born there. She was the first English child born in America. Were Virginia and the other settlers captured by Native Americans? Did they die of starvation? Did they migrate to another colony? No one knows.

Before their ship landed, members of Plymouth Colony signed an agreement to set up a government of laws. This was the beginning of democracy in the New World.

(left) These costumed interpreters at Jamestown Settlement in Virginia portray life during the 1600s.

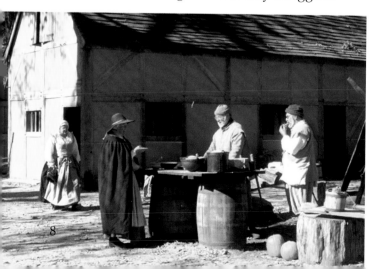

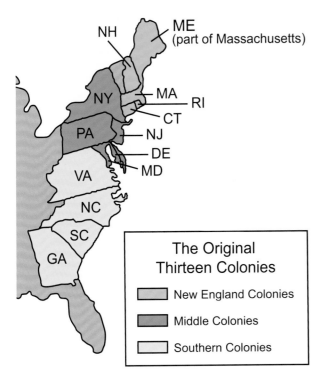

NH

ME (part of Massachusetts)

NY
MA
RI
CT
PA
NJ
DE
MD
VA
NC
SC
GA

The Original Thirteen Colonies

New England Colonies

Middle Colonies

Southern Colonies

(left) The thirteen colonies were founded between 1607 and 1752.

(below) Plymouth Rock—where the Mayflower and the Pilgrims landed in 1620

Massachusetts

The people who founded the first colonies in New England were searching not for wealth, but for religious freedom. Puritans and Separatists were devout Christians who wanted to worship in ways that the Church of England, the official church, did not allow. They risked a perilous ocean voyage to gain religious freedom. In 1620, about 100 Separatists sailed for North America on the Mayflower. They landed at a place they called Plymouth. Soon after, Puritans began settlements at Salem and Boston. The three towns would join with others to become the colony of Massachusetts.

Religious freedom

Puritan leaders in Massachusetts, surprisingly, were not accepting of those who did not believe as they did. People mistreated by the Puritans moved to more tolerant colonies such as Rhode Island, New Netherland (later called New York), and Pennsylvania. Pennsylvania became a special haven, or shelter, for Quakers, a religious group that was **persecuted** in Great Britain and other countries. Meanwhile, both Catholics and Protestants were welcome in the colony of Maryland.

William Penn founded the colony of Pennsylvania where Quakers and others could worship freely.

Slavery

As in Virginia, people in Maryland and the other Southern Colonies grew tobacco, as well as rice. The wealthiest farmers owned huge farms called plantations. They purchased large numbers of enslaved Africans to plant, weed, and harvest their crops. Slavery was less common in the Middle Colonies—Pennsylvania, New Jersey, and New York. People there mainly grew wheat or raised livestock on smaller farms. In rocky New England, most people lived on small farms close to a town, but farming was much less important to the economy than fishing and industries such as shipbuilding and timbering. Slavery took hold much more strongly in the South because of these regional differences.

9

New land, new government

From the start, the English colonists were concerned about creating fair governments. The men who arrived on the Mayflower signed a compact, or agreement, to create "just and equal laws" for all. As people settled in towns, they chose town leaders by voting. In order to vote, a person had to be male and own a certain amount of property. Each colony also had its own government. The governor and other top officials were appointed by the English king, but the colonists elected representatives to an assembly, which helped make laws for the colony.

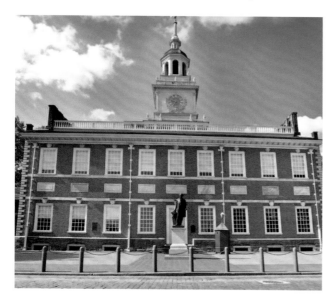

(above) Both the Declaration of Independence and the Constitution were signed in Philadelphia at the Pennsylvania State House, now known as Independence Hall.

Stricter British rule

In the 1760s after its costly war with France in North America, Great Britain began to place stricter laws on the American colonies. One law **prohibited** settlement west of the Appalachian Mountains. Other laws imposed taxes on imported goods such as molasses, paint, glass, and paper, and placed British troops in parts of the colonies. The Stamp Act of 1765 called for a tax on newspapers and all kinds of legal documents. The colonists made strong protests against these laws. Many viewed them as unjust because Americans had no voice in Parliament, England's **legislature.** A tax on tea in 1773 led to bolder acts of protest.

The American Revolution

April 1775 brought a deadly skirmish with British troops in Massachusetts. Colonial leaders now felt their only choice was to declare American independence. In the five-year war from 1776 to 1781, the Americans, aided in the end by the French, were victorious. The U.S. Constitution went into effect in 1788 and by 1790 had been **ratified** by all original 13 colonies. A key part of this document is the Bill of Rights, which was ratified in 1791. It guarantees important rights, such as freedom of speech, religion, and the press.

(below) No taxation without representation was the cry of many colonists who protested British policies.

Americans chose George Washington for their first president. Washington served as commander in chief of the Continental Army during the war for American independence. He was known for his strong moral character and modesty.

Adding territory

Until 1801, the western limit of the United States was the Mississippi River. Thomas Jefferson, the third U.S. president, doubled the size of the nation. From France, he purchased the vast sweep of land between the river and the Rocky Mountains for $15 million. The area was called the Louisiana Purchase.

In 1804, Jefferson sent a team of explorers into this wilderness. Their job was to make maps, talk with Native Americans, and write reports on the plants, animals, and rocks they found. Meriwether Lewis and William Clark led the expedition, which followed the Missouri River from St. Louis. They crossed the mountains and traveled all the way to the Pacific Ocean. Their discoveries stirred growing interest in the West.

This statue in Indiana commemorates the work of Lewis and Clark.

(below) Chinese gold miners in California

A nation on the move

Between 1800 and 1850, the United States grew in size and population. New towns, cities, and states were founded. Hundreds of thousands of farmers migrated to the far West in covered wagons. A gold rush in California drew miners from as far away as China. Meanwhile waves of **immigrants** from Europe swelled the size of eastern cities. In the Northeast, more people, including women and children, began to work in mechanized mills and factories.

Better roads, a network of railroads, and a system of canals in the Northeast, improved transportation and trade. Steam-powered boats and trains became more common. People, products, and raw materials could travel faster and farther than ever before.

Eastern tribes

As land-hungry farmers moved west, Native Americans responded. Some groups began to adopt the ways of white society. For example, the Cherokee, a large tribe in the Southeast, created a system of writing and a government with elections, courts, and a constitution. Other groups did not want to **assimilate.** In 1812, Chief Tecumseh organized the tribes of the Ohio River Valley to fight the advance of white settlers. Tecumseh and his allies were defeated, and in 1838 the U.S. government forced all Cherokee to move to Indian Territory in what is now Oklahoma.

A nation divided

By 1860, the northern and southern states had developed very different economies. In the South, cotton was now "king," and four million slaves provided free labor on plantations. In the North, **manufacturing** was much more important, and people flocked to towns and cities to work in factories and shops for wages. Strict laws in the South ensured that enslaved people remained enslaved. In the North, however, many people viewed slavery as morally wrong, and in most states it was illegal. Many sharp words were exchanged in Congress on the issue of slavery. In 1861, the slave states of the deep South chose to **secede.** They withdrew from the Union and formed a new government called the Confederacy. This action sparked the beginning of the Civil War.

(top) An African-American soldier guards a cannon during the Civil War.

(below) Life during the Civil War was hard. Occasionally families joined the troops to cook and do laundry for the soldiers.

The end of slavery

After four years of dreadful warfare, mostly in the South, the Confederacy surrendered. Between 1865 and 1877, the reunited nation went through a period called Reconstruction. Feelings of bitterness among southern whites lingered a long time, and much work was needed to help former slaves take control of their future. Three amendments were added to the Constitution to protect the rights of African Americans. The Thirteenth Amendment banned slavery throughout the United States. The Fourteenth Amendment gave full citizenship to former slaves. The Fifteenth Amendment gave African Americans the right to vote.

President Abraham Lincoln, in a stovepipe hat, frequently met with his generals, sometimes on the battlefield.

The modern United States

After the Civil War, the United States became an industrial giant and an international military power. Women, African Americans, and immigrants all played a part in shaping the rapidly growing nation.

An industrial boom

In the late 1850s inventions such as the telephone, electric lightbulb, and streetcars made living and working easier. A new process for making steel stronger gave rise to a booming steel industry. Using steel, workers built railroads, bridges, ships, skyscrapers, and new kinds of machines used to manufacture countless products. Oil, first discovered in Pennsylvania, greased the wheels of industry. Some businesses became huge and their owners extremely rich. Andrew Carnegie owned most of America's steel mills. John D. Rockefeller, head of the Standard Oil Company, had a **monopoly** in the oil industry.

The United States had plenty of people eager to work in its factories and mills. Between 1870 and 1916, newcomers and new births doubled the population. Wages, especially for unskilled jobs, were low, and workers were fired for injury or illness. Workplaces were commonly dirty, smelly, and dangerous. Yet workers were very

productive. By 1900, the United States was the leading industrial nation in the world. Shop owners, factory managers, sales clerks, and office workers were also important in the growing workforce. They were considered members of the middle class. They lived in comfortable homes and enjoyed entertainments such as going to amusement parks, reading magazines, or playing their own parlor pianos.

Growing cities

Immigrants, hoping for jobs that would lead to a better life, swarmed into big cities such as New York, Chicago, and Philadelphia. Most could only afford to live in crowded, poorly-built **tenements** in neighborhoods that lacked clean water and sewers. Immigrants from the same country lived near each other for friendship and support. People who had grown up on farms and African Americans from the South also migrated to northern cities. By the end of the century, a growing 40 percent of Americans lived in cities.

(top) For decades women fought for the right to vote. Members of the National American Woman Suffrage Association held parades and marched in support of gaining voting rights.

(left) Many poor families could survive only if all members of the family earned money.

Reform, struggles, and strife

The terrible working conditions in factories and living conditions in city slums sparked a reform movement, as groups organized to help improve people's lives. Factory workers formed **unions** to press business owners for better pay and safer working conditions. Progressives, people who had ideas about ways to fix American society, felt that the national government should take the lead in bringing about reforms. President Theodore Roosevelt was a Progressive. He used lawsuits to keep businesses from getting too powerful and sided with Pennsylvania coal miners when they went on strike. He also urged Congress to pass the Food and Drug Act, which made meat processed in factories safer to eat.

Educated middle-class women were very active in the Progressive movement, especially in demanding suffrage, or the right to vote. The suffragists faced much opposition, but in 1920 the Nineteenth Amendment giving women the right to vote was ratified.

African Americans made strides in education. Many adults and children in the South learned to read and write. In the North, some middle-class African Americans attended college.

In 1848 the Declaration of Rights and Sentiments called for equal rights for women. It would be more than 70 years later before the right to vote was won.

However, African Americans as a whole struggled. In the South, local laws, special fees, and threats of violence prevented African Americans from voting. **Segregation** prevented African Americans from attending the same schools, restaurants, and churches as whites. After 1900, Progressives turned their attention to these problems by forming organizations such as the National Association for the Advancement of Colored People, to fight for racial equality.

As the lives of African Americans were improving, at least in some small ways, conditions for Native Americans worsened. In the West, the government was fighting the last of the Indian Wars. Survivors were pushed onto **reservations**, where they were required to become farmers. These changes disrupted Native culture and caused deep feelings of hopelessness among many Native people. Further, Native Americans were not granted the right to vote until 1924 when the Indian Citizenship Act was passed.

(left) Chief Joseph of the Nez Perce resisted movement to a reservation in Idaho before finally making peace with the U.S. government.

World War I

A great destructive war that involved most of the nations of Europe broke out in 1914. The United States fought on the side of Great Britain, France, and their **allies** against powerful Germany and its allies. When World War I began, the United States hoped to remain neutral. In 1917, after German submarines began sinking U.S. merchant ships, President Woodrow Wilson asked Congress to declare war on Germany. The war ended in victory for America and its allies but left much of Europe in ruins and politically unstable.

African American jazz musicians and jazz orchestras, like this one led by Duke Ellington, were popular with American audiences of all races.

Good times

For many Americans, the 1920s were a time of prosperity. They could afford new time-saving appliances such as vacuum cleaners and washing machines and even one of Henry Ford's mass-produced cars. In their free time, Americans listened to music, baseball games, and comedy shows on the radio and went to the movies. In cities, they danced to live bands that played the brassy, **syncopated** music called jazz.

Harlem, an African-American neighborhood in New York City, was the heart of the new music scene. African American writers, artists, actors, and playwrights were also drawn to Harlem. These men and women were the core of a broad flowering of African-American talent and pride known as the Harlem Renaissance.

During the Great Depression, breadlines, where free food was distributed to the unemployed and hungry, were organized in many cities.

Hard times

Although the 1920s were considered a boom time, serious problems began to develop in the nation's economy. Factories were producing less, lower crop prices had put many farmers in debt, and banks and individuals were putting much of their money into risky stock-market investments. By 1932, these problems combined to produce the Great Depression, the nation's worst economic slowdown. In the 1930s, countless banks and businesses closed, and as many as one in four people was unemployed. Many of the jobless became homeless. In every city hungry people stood in long lines for handouts of soup and bread.

President Franklin D. Roosevelt and Congress launched a massive relief program, called the New Deal, to help put the nation back to work. In addition, new government agencies were created to better regulate banking and the stock market.

World War II

In World War II, many countries around the world fought to keep Nazi leader Adolph Hitler of Germany and other dictators from taking over Europe and Asia. The United States joined the war in 1940 after Japan, an ally of Germany, bombed the U.S. Navy base in Pearl Harbor, Hawaii. In 1945, President Truman approved the use of a powerful new weapon called the atomic bomb on Japan. The war ended soon after.

A new enemy

After World War II, the Soviet Union, the first **Communist** nation, occupied countries in eastern Europe and East Asia, setting up anti-democratic governments. A long period of mistrust between the United States and the Soviet Union, known as the Cold War, followed. The two countries came into conflict in the war in Vietnam. U.S. forces fought unsuccessfully to keep Communist North Vietnam from taking over South Vietnam. The United States and the Soviet Union continued to compete for power and stockpile nuclear arms until the breakup of the Soviet Union in 1991.

Women and men, black and white, marched peacefully in cities and towns throughout the South and in Washington, D.C., to demand equal rights and an end to segregation in the United States.

Rights for African Americans

In the 1950s and 1960s, African Americans, along with many concerned whites, took action to end unjust laws and discrimination in jobs, housing, and education. Demonstrators used peaceful forms of protest to draw attention to racial injustice. The steady stream of courageous demonstrations led Congress to pass a series of important **civil rights** laws in the 1960s, including the Voting Rights Act and the Fair Housing Act. During this time, Mexican Americans and Native Americans also stood up for equal rights.

The United States today

The United States is still a leading economic power. In particular, American inventiveness in computer technology has transformed how people communicate and work. Using laptops, smart phones, and video conferencing, many people now work from home. Service industries, such as health care and finance, remain important in the economy, but many traditional manufacturing jobs have been lost to countries such as China and India.

A key challenge today is international terrorism. On September 11, 2001, a small group of terrorists **hijacked** four passenger planes in the United States. The terrorists crashed two planes into the World Trade Center in New York City and one into the Pentagon, the nation's defense headquarters in Washington, D.C. Passengers on a fourth plane forced it to crash into the ground in Pennsylvania. In response, the U.S. government took military actions in Afghanistan and Iraq. It also formed the Department of Homeland Security to keep the nation safer from terrorist threats.

(below) After the events of 9/11, travelers must follow stricter rules and endure more thorough screenings at airports.

Americans all

The United States has long been described as a nation of immigrants. Some came generations ago, while others have just arrived. The population of America is a changing tapestry of many threads.

Waves of immigrants

The English settlers who formed the thirteen colonies were soon joined by immigrants from Scotland, Ireland, and Germany. A second wave of immigration, mainly from northern and western Europe, began in the early 1800s and lasted through the Civil War. A third and much bigger flow of newcomers—from countries such as Italy, Poland, Greece, and Russia—occurred between the 1880s and 1920. Immigration picked up again after 1965, with most new people coming from Asia and Latin America.

In the 1600s, Spanish people began to move into the Southwest from Mexico. Throughout the history of the United States, many people have walked, ridden, and driven across the Mexican border to live in Texas, California, Arizona, as well as in other states. Immigrants today continue to come to the United States to find a better life, and they continue to enrich the culture and the economy of the nation.

Traditions, food, and language

Many traditions observed in the United States began with different immigrant groups. The first English settlers started the custom of enjoying a bountiful harvest dinner at Thanksgiving. From the Germans who settled in Pennsylvania comes the custom of celebrating Christmas with a decorated tree. Cinco de Mayo is celebrated throughout the Southwest, and Chinese New Year celebrations occur in a number of cities across the nation.

This multi-generational Hispanic-American family lives in Tucson, Arizona.

These people are practicing tai chi, a form of slow-moving exercise that focuses the mind, at a park in New York City.

San Francisco has the largest Asian-American population of any city in the United States.

These new American citizens are taking an oath of allegiance to the United States. They come from more than a dozen countries including Burma, Pakistan, Morocco, and the United Kingdom.

In addition, the foods Americans enjoy, both at home and in restaurants, reflect the cuisines of many nations. Mexican food such as tacos, which are corn tortillas filled with beans or meat, are extremely popular all over the United States. Chinese dishes often feature stir-fried vegetables and meat served with rice. Middle Eastern falafel are fried balls of ground chickpeas. Greek gyros are sandwiches of lamb on pita bread. Indian dahl is a sauce made of spiced lentils. All of these foods have a place on American tables.

Over 300 years, the influx of people from other countries has also added many new words to the English language. Here are three examples: *canyon* (Spanish), *bouquet* (French), *caddy* (Gaelic/Scotland). Can you think of others?

 # City life, country life

The vast landscape of the United States is peppered with small towns and large cities. Every state, however, still has open land that is used for farming or, in the West, for ranching.

Spreading cities

Many cities in the United States sprang up near waterways that people used for transportation and trade. In the 1900s, cities became centers of industry. During this time, the electric trolley car allowed many people to live in pleasant suburbs and **commute** to work. Today, both people and businesses have spread out even farther, into surrounding farmland. This has caused the oldest parts of many big cities to decline. In many places, this trend is changing. "Urban pioneers" are restoring rundown neighborhoods, and local governments are taking steps to make cities more inviting to both residents and tourists.

Chicago and Houston

Chicago, Illinois, and Houston, Texas, are the third and fourth largest cities in the nation. Houston, Texas, boomed after vast supplies of oil were discovered in east Texas in the early 1900s. Today, many Houston residents work in gleaming office towers owned by the world's largest oil companies or in various oil-related businesses. People also come downtown for fun—to enjoy fine restaurants, go to museums and theaters, and to watch the city's professional football and baseball teams.

Chicago was one of the first large cities in the Midwest. Hugging Lake Michigan, the city has long been a transportation hub. Its diverse businesses include finance and insurance, printing and publishing, and food processing. Many Chicago residents live in high-rise apartment buildings. They enjoy Chicago's beautiful waterfront, relaxing parks, handsome skyscrapers, and fine museums.

Houston is one of the largest cities in the Southwest. The city sprawls over 8,778 square miles (22,735 sq km), and with its suburbs encompasses 12,475 square miles (32,310 sq km).

(top) Chicago's Willis Tower is the tallest skyscraper in the United States. Chicagoans and tourists alike can find many recreational activities downtown at Grant Park, which faces Lake Michigan.

Farms and ranches

Many country dwellers live in houses located on an acre or two of land, and they drive to urban areas to work. Some rural Americans, however, make their living from the land. In soil-rich states such as Illinois and Nebraska, many farmers grow wheat or corn. A typical farm family lives in a house that is close to barns, silos, equipment sheds, or other outbuildings. Teenage children are generally expected to help with chores. Farm work can be tiring, especially in the spring and fall, but it has been made easier by modern equipment.

(below) While cattle require less daily care than other farm animals, they still have to be fed. Here a rancher puts out hay for his herd of cattle.

(above) These farm workers are harvesting wheat with a combine. The cab offers air-conditioning and a radio, which make the long job more pleasant.

In dry grassland states such as Texas and Colorado, cattle, sheep, and goats are raised on large ranches. The work routine on a cattle ranch follows the seasons. Young calves are branded in the spring and rounded up in the fall for market. In the summer, ranchers mend fences, check water supplies, and look after the animals' health. Most ranchers use trucks and four-wheelers for these chores, rather than horses. Even with mechanized tractors, plows, and other farm machinery, the workdays can be long, and work on a farm is never-ending.

The armed forces

The men and women who serve in the U.S. armed forces have a double duty—to fight the nation's enemies and to defend the nation's interests when they are threatened. The five branches of the U.S. military are the army, the navy, the air force, the Marine Corps, and the Coast Guard. The army began during the American Revolution and is the oldest and largest branch. The Marines work closely with the navy to make forceful, leading attacks on the ground and from the air.

Training

People who enter the military must be at least 17 years old. New recruits go through a training period that is physically and mentally challenging. The knowledge and discipline they gain help them perform as part of a team in stressful situations. In the army, recruits then go to school to learn a specialty such as vehicle repair; managing supplies; or using a particular type of weapon, such as a tank. Many people in the military serve in noncombat posts such as translating, nursing, and intelligence, which is gathering and analyzing strategic information.

(below) Basic training for Marines is physically and mentally challenging. In addition to demanding physical fitness drills, Marines also learn to march in formation.

A soldier is welcomed home by his wife after returning from a tour of duty in Iraq.

Serving

During the Civil War, the world wars, the Korean War, and the Vietnam War, the national government imposed a draft. It required all men to enroll for possible selection into the military. Since 1973, enlisting in the armed services has been voluntary. In times of peace, members of the armed services are often called on to perform **humanitarian** missions. For example, in 2005, several branches of the military helped to protect the lives and property of Hurricane Katrina victims in New Orleans. Military forces brought in needed food supplies and dropped sandbags to hold back flooding.

In the United States, families and friends gather for personal celebrations such as birthdays and weddings. These events happen in different ways depending on the cultural background of the families, as well as personal choice.

Special birthdays

In some cultures, birthdays that are thought to mark the transition from child to adult are celebrated in special ways. Among Hispanic Americans, for example, many 15-year-old girls are honored with a *quinceañera* (keen-say-ah-NYAIR-ah), a ceremony that started centuries ago. This event centers around a Mass of thanksgiving, a religious service that takes place in a Catholic church. The girl wears a beautiful gown, a symbol of her maturity, and is attended by well-dressed girls and boys of similar age. The mass is often followed by a banquet for family and friends that includes music, dancing, and an oversized cake.

Among Jews, boys become full members of their religious community at age 13 and girls at age 12. This means they are required to live by the commandments of Judaism. The crossing over to religious adulthood is often marked with a ceremony in a **synagogue.** The boy or girl reads a portion of the *Torah* (the first five books of the Hebrew Bible) or says a blessing in Hebrew before gathered relatives and friends. After the service, guests attend a party hosted by the parents.

Getting married

Among the multicultural population of the United States, wedding celebrations can vary widely. Some couples marry in the church that the bride or groom or both belong to. Other couples choose to be married by a judge, in a public place or at home. A bride often wears a white gown and carries a bouquet of flowers, while the groom wears a suit. The two recite their **vows** for all attending to hear, and they exchange rings as a sign of their love and commitment.

(left) This young man reads from the Torah *during his Bar Mitzvah, the ceremony marking his transition to adulthood in the Jewish faith.*

(below) June is a popular month for weddings. This couple is getting married in a local park.

The first settlers ate the same foods as the Native Americans, and Native Americans showed them what was safe to eat. Foods included wild nuts and berries; meat from woodland animals such as rabbits, deer, and turkeys; fish and shellfish from local rivers and the sea; and Indian corn and squash, which could be grown on small patches of ground. In the 1700s, American colonists sat down to meals that might feature roast lamb, bacon, hot biscuits and butter, peanut soup, cornmeal mush, or mince pies filled with chopped meat, apples, raisins, and spices. Families honor this bounty by gathering for a large feast in late November on the national holiday of Thanksgiving. A traditional Thanksgiving menu is roast turkey, mashed potatoes with gravy, cooked green beans, and pumpkin pie for dessert. The United States today is still a land of plentiful food.

All-American foods

Although there is a saying, "as American as apple pie," hot dogs, hamburgers, popcorn, and ice cream probably rank as America's favorite foods. Hot dogs and hamburgers are cooked on the grill at outdoor picnics. Popcorn is a favorite snack when watching videos at home. In summer, people line up at ice cream stands and shops to consider thirty or more flavors before ordering a scoop or two in a cone. Ice cream served in cones has been popular in America ever since the 1904 World's Fair in St. Louis, Missouri.

Three meals a day

Breakfast on weekdays is often simple: cold cereal, toast, and milk or orange juice. On the weekend, some people take time to enjoy a hot breakfast with pancakes and syrup or scrambled eggs with sausage or bacon. Children are given nutritious lunches at school, with typical fare such as a peanut-butter-and-jelly sandwich and carrot sticks, or pasta with

These two girls enjoy a summertime favorite—ice cream cones.

tomato sauce and a salad, or they bring a packed lunch from home. Evening meals are different for each family. Some parents make many meals "from scratch," while others rely on convenience foods such as canned soup, biscuit mixes, or frozen dinners. Most cities and towns have a large number of restaurants. Friday night, at the end of the workweek, is a popular time for going out to eat.

Fast food

The United States is known around the world for its many fast-food chains, such as MacDonald's and KFC (Kentucky Fried Chicken). Fast food is especially popular with young people. A classic American fast-food meal is a hamburger, French-fried potatoes, and a soft drink such as Pepsi or Coca-Cola. Pizza and

Family members gather together for an evening dinner of chicken, vegetables, and rolls. Sitting down together at dinner gives them a chance to relax, to catch up and talk about the day's events, and to discuss what tomorrow might bring.

tacos are also favorites. Fast food is inexpensive and tasty but is usually high in calories, fat, and salt, and low in vitamins, minerals, and fiber. The popularity of fast food, for both meals and snacks, is one factor in the rise of child and adult **obesity** in the United States. In recent years, however, restaurant chains have been making serious efforts to offer healthier, lower calories meals, and these are becoming popular choices for customers of all ages.

Healthy food

In recent years, more and more Americans have become aware of the importance of eating healthy foods. The government has recommended a "Food Plate," which consists of equal portions of fruit, grains, vegetables, and protein (which includes lean meat and beans), and servings of low-fat dairy products, with only very small amounts of fats, oil, and sweets. Farm markets that offer fresh, local produce are now common in cities across the nation. In addition, farms close to urban areas have started services in which they deliver seasonal, fresh fruit and vegetables to individual homes every week. People are buying locally grown produce in their supermarkets, and they are eating more fruits and vegetables. They are also choosing healthier snacks, such as cheese, yogurt, or granola bars.

These neighborhood friends are enjoying a traditional summer barbecue with hamburgers, watermelon, and fresh corn-on-the-cob.

Sports and games

In the United States, spectator sports including auto racing, baseball, and football, are very popular, but so is playing sports yourself. Reading, listening to music, watching television, playing computer games, and going out to see the newest movies are some other ways that Americans have fun.

Automobile racing

Stock car automobile racing is a huge spectator sport, and many of the races are sponsored by the National Association for Stock Car Auto Racing (NASCAR). It is estimated that more than 50 million people worldwide are NASCAR fans. Millions of fans in the United States watch the Daytona 500, held at the Daytona International Speedway in Florida, and close to 150,000 people attend this annual event. In Indiana, the Indianapolis Motor Speedway, home of the Indianapolis 500, can accommodate more than 250,000 fans.

(below) Baseball has been called America's national pastime, and thousands of fans come out every summer evening to root for their home team. A baseball game lasts for nine innings, usually three or four hours.

The Indianapolis 500 attracts top drivers from all over the world. The first Indy 500 was held in 1911 with 40 cars reaching speeds over 70 mph (113 km/h).

Baseball in the summer

In baseball, two teams of nine players take turns playing in the field and "at bat." The players at bat try to hit the ball so the other team cannot get to it, then try to run around the four bases that are laid out in a diamond pattern on the field. A player reaching the last base, or "home," scores a point. An exciting moment in baseball is when a batter hits the ball out of the **stadium** to instantly score a home run. Baseball is less popular than it used to be, but every fall millions of television spectators tune in for the World Series—a match between the champions of the American and National Leagues.

(left) Professional football is a major sports industry with millions of fans. Here the Cincinnati Bengals play against the Indianapolis Colts on a sunny Sunday afternoon. The football season ends in February with the Super Bowl, when the top team from the AFC (American Football Conference) plays against the top team from the NFC (National Football Conference).

Football in the fall

Football is a contact sport, so players wear helmets and protective padding. It is played on a marked field 100 yards long with goal posts at each end. In a series of short plays, one team runs with the ball or throws a pass to try to advance down the field toward the goal. A player who carries the ball across the goal line scores a touchdown. The other team tries to prevent this by tackling the runner or knocking down passes, and stealing the ball if it can. Football is played from early fall to mid-winter.

"Hoops"

Basketball is a fast-moving indoor sport played on a court by two teams of five players. Each team tries to score points by throwing or dunking a large inflated ball through a high hoop at each end of the court. Players dribble, or bounce, the ball as they advance and make quick passes to teammates, while opposing players closely guard them. Basketball is played in high schools and colleges. Many cities also have professional teams, such as the Miami Heat and the Detroit Pistons. Basketball is also viewed as a fun way to get exercise. On paved driveways at homes and on neighborhood courts, children, teens, and adults like to shoot hoops and play one on one.

Many boys who are good at basketball dream of playing in the NBA (National Basketball Association) someday. Women also play professional basketball. The Women's National Basketball Association was organized in 1996 and now has 12 teams in major cities across the nation.

Computer games

American teenagers enjoy computer games, and those who like them play nearly every day. Racing and puzzle games are very popular. Realistic action games, which often involve sports, adventure, or warfare, tend to be favored more by boys. For these games, users hold a console in two hands to control the action on a video screen. In some longer games, players invent and then role-play heroic characters who perform fantastic feats in a story they make up as they go along. Teens play computer games alone and with friends, in person and online, on home computers and on small hand-held devices.

Keeping fit

Many boys, girls, and adults take part in summertime softball leagues. Softball has rules similar to baseball but uses a larger ball and underhand pitching. Soccer is another team sport that many young people are drawn to. For exercise, some adults and teens do aerobic dance routines to music, while others prefer quieter forms of exercise such as jogging or hiking. The United States has magnificent national and state parks where people go to hike, fish, and camp overnight.

Playing computer games is a popular after-school activity for many young people.

(below) This couple takes time to exercise together, jogging in a public park. Many public parks have jogging trails, tennis courts, and planned outdoor exercise stations.

When most Americans still lived on farms, children of all ages walked to one-room schoolhouses. The core subjects were reading, penmanship, and arithmetic. Older students were often paired with younger ones to help them learn. Students attended school only part of the year during times when they could be spared from farm chores. Many did not go beyond eighth grade.

Making the grade

Today, every state requires girls and boys to go to school, but the laws for when they can start and end their schooling vary. The most common pattern is to begin school at age five with kindergarten. Then, students complete five or six years of elementary school, two years of junior high, and then go on to high school, which covers grades 9 through 12.

Required subjects in high school usually include English, history, math, and science. Students also choose and take additional subjects. Many learn a second language, which helps them discover how people in another culture live and think. **Extracurricular** activities add to the school experience. Students can join **choral** groups or clubs, play team sports, or perform in school plays.

Public and private schools

Most American students attend public school, which is free. Public schools exist in every community in the nation, and they are funded through taxes paid by local citizens. Some parents choose to send their children to charter schools. These are public schools with a specific design. They may focus on certain kinds of students, such as English language learners;

Science is taught at all levels of school, from elementary through high school. Students often work together in labs to explore, to test, and to discover.

Colleges and universities attract students from every state in the nation and from foreign countries, as well. Students have opportunities to learn from each other in informal settings and from their professors in traditional classrooms and laboratories.

certain subjects, such as math and science; or certain teaching methods. Another option is home schooling, where parents teach their children directly. All these kinds of schooling must meet requirements set by the state.

About 10 percent of students go to private schools, for which they pay fees, called tuition. Most private-school students attend Catholic or other church-sponsored schools close to home. Some students from wealthier families go to boarding schools, where they live and study.

After high school

High-school graduates can continue their education in several ways. Four-year colleges offer a broad education. Students get degrees in the arts and sciences, such as history, biology, or art. Community colleges tend to focus on preparing people for jobs, and many offer two-year degrees. Graduates might become chefs, dental assistants, or auto mechanics. Universities are similar to colleges but have graduate schools where people can earn advanced degrees to become teachers, doctors, lawyers, engineers, and scientists. All of these kinds of schools charge tuition.

Students often work independently on online courses.

Excellence in education

The United States has many fine colleges and universities—large and small, public and private. One of the oldest and most respected is Harvard University in Cambridge, Massachusetts. Eight presidents have studied there, including John Adams, John F. Kennedy, and Barack Obama. Many state universities are important research centers. For example, a physicist at the University of California Berkeley, along with two others, won a Nobel Prize in 2011 for an important discovery about how the universe is expanding.

Jenna's busy day

As Jenna sat at the breakfast table, her mother set a bowl of oatmeal with melting brown sugar on it in front of her. Jenna was busy tapping out a message to her friend Brad on her cell phone: *sounds good cu sat.*

"Jenna, no texting at meals—remember?" Her mother said.

"Oops, sorry," Jenna said, as she slipped her cell phone into her jeans pocket. "I was messaging Brad back about the riverside cleanup on Saturday." Her mother smiled.

Jenna, a seventh-grade student, and her mom live in a small town outside Columbus, Ohio, the state capital. She walks to the junior high school in their town, which is close to a scenic river called the Big Darby Creek.

It was Thursday. After finishing breakfast, Jenna fed her dog, Loopy. Her mother, who works in a hospital admissions office, packed lunches for both of them.

Jenna's school day begins at 8 a.m. and ends at 3 p.m. She always arrives early so she can talk with friends in the hall and get the book she needs for her first class from her locker. When the bell rings, she heads toward her English

1:00 p.m. Jenna learns to use a sewing machine in her home economics class. She wants to learn to make items and donate them to charity.

class, her favorite. Her other main classes are earth science, home economics, and math. This year, she is also taking beginning band to learn how to play the flute.

After school, Jenna and Brad headed for the community center where their 4-H club meets each month. 4-H is a national organization of clubs that helps young people learn life and citizenship skills. Their own club, called Helping Hands, focuses on service projects.

At the meeting, the club advisor, Mr. Chenski, reviewed what everyone will do at the Saturday cleanup. Parents will lead teams of four students in collecting trash along different parts of the riverbank. Each person will have a large plastic bag for gathering paper and other lightweight trash. Anything big, such as old tires or rusty junk, will be loaded by adults into pickup trucks or canoes. After three hours, everyone will meet at the canoe launch for a picnic lunch.

(left) 7:00 a.m. Jenna messages Brad asking if he is still going to the riverside cleanup on Saturday.

It was about 5 p.m. when Jenna walked through her front door and greeted her mom, who was already home from her job. As they ate supper together, Jenna talked excitedly about the Saturday cleanup. Afterward, she rinsed the dishes and put them in the dishwasher. Then she refilled the dog's water bowl. Now it was time to practice her flute and do her homework, which she normally does right after school.

Jenna was done by around 8 p.m. That gave her time to read her library book and then surf the Web for a while on the family computer. A video she discovered at the 4-H website for another state made her pause. High school students dressed as clowns and wearing paint on their faces were doing goofy stunts and singing funny songs for a group of people at a nursing home. Everyone was smiling. Quickly, Jenna copied the video link into an e-mail to Brad. Then she typed: *How about this for our next project? I think it would be a lot of fun!*

Saturday. Jenna, Brad and the other 4-H club volunteers collected 16 bags of garbage from the riverbank.

6:45 p.m. After supper, Jenna's mom helps her do her math homework. Tomorrow will be another busy day!

Glossary

allies Countries that agree to help one another

assimilate Blend into the customs of a group of people, or be absorbed by a group of people

choral Singing

civil rights Rights that every citizen of a particular country should have

colonial Relating to the time period before the 13 colonies formed the United States

colonies Areas controlled by a distant country

commute Travel back and forth regularly, usually to a place of work or to school

Communist Refers to a system of government in which all the land and factories belong to the government and are shared by everyone

diverse Different from one another, varied

earthworks Raised banks or walls made of soil

economy System or process for making choices about how goods and services are produced, bought, and sold

export Goods sent to and sold to other countries

extracurricular Activities that can be done at school, but that are not part of the regular schedule of classes

hijacked Stolen, taking an airplane by force or by forcing the driver of an automobile to give up control of the vehicle

humanitarian Working to make other people's lives better

immigrants People who move to another country to live

legislature A group of people who make or pass laws

manufacturing Making things by machine or by hand

monopoly Complete control by one provider of a particular good or service

nomadic Roaming from place to place, with no established home

obesity Overweight in a very unhealthy way

persecuted Attacked or treated unfairly because of one's beliefs, religion, or race

prohibited Not allowed, prevented

ratified Officially approved

reservations Areas of land set aside by the federal government for Native Americans to live on

secede Withdraw from a country and become independent

segregation Keeping people of a different race, sex, or social class away from others

stadium A large, usually open, area where sports, like football or baseball, are played

synagogue A building that is used as a house of prayer for Jewish people

syncopated Unexpected musical rhythm that stresses the normally weak beats instead of the strong beats

tenements High-rise apartment buildings where many families live in crowded conditions

tribes Groups of people with the same customs, language, and relatives

unions Organizations that form to fight for improvement of working conditions, wages, and benefits

vows Important or sacred promises that people make to each other

Index